# Findings

# Findings

*Poems by Meg Kennedy*

Poems copyright © 2023 by Meg Kennedy
All rights reserved
Printed in the United States of America
First Edition

Published by

BookArts Press
www.book-arts-press.com
ISBN 978-0-9795861-7-0

*Attention, taken to its highest degree,
is the same thing as prayer.*

*--Simone Weil*

Preface................................................................ix

# I ...................................................................... 1

Broken Glass.................................................. 3
Pottery Lesson ............................................... 5
Vessel ............................................................. 7
Fault Lines ..................................................... 9
Empty Nest................................................... 11
Crows............................................................ 13
That Fall....................................................... 15
October Metallurgy...................................... 17
November .................................................... 19
Thaw............................................................. 21
Japanese Maple in February........................ 23

# II ................................................................... 25

Beachcombing ............................................. 27
Making Marks.............................................. 29
Cicada Song................................................. 31
Psalm of Stone............................................. 33
Shedding...................................................... 35
My Yellow Room ......................................... 37
Writing ........................................................ 39
Autumn Litany............................................ 41
Lessons........................................................ 43

# III ................................................................. 45

Getting Found............................................. 47
Nest.............................................................. 49
Last Walk .................................................... 51
Extension..................................................... 53
Our Garden ................................................. 55
Spring Inspiration ....................................... 57
As the Crow Flies........................................ 59

About the Author ............................................ 61
Colophon ......................................................... 63

# Preface

For fifty years I've written poems. At first as assignments for a creative writing major (because I wanted to make the big bucks), but later, after abandoning adolescent hopes of discovery as the next Sylvia Plath and joining the real world, I continued to write for myself. In assembling this collection I discovered (and discarded) work that I once thought profound but which no longer resonated, work that I still loved, and pieces that were merely drafts of what they were meant to be.

Also I found reasons why I continue to write: to celebrate moments; to check in on how I'm doing; to reflect on my surroundings; and to address issues that concern me. So I chose the title, *Findings*. Now, entering my eighth decade, collecting this poetry into a book is another check on my bucket list, but not an end to my writing. In addition to examining the sources of these poems, I found that my love of words, playful descriptions, and intense focus on the minutia that makes up the whole are still my way of reacting to the everyday. This lifelong attraction to writing words led to and nurtured my career as a professional calligrapher and book artist.

Any acknowledgment for a collection of never-published writing is pointless, but thanks are definitely in order. I am most grateful to Liz Chang for her friendship, encouragement, and editorial guidance; and to Jon Pastor, my husband and partner in life, for designing and publishing this work and for allowing use of his beautiful cover photograph. Thanks also to friends along the way who have been willing to read this or that poem and to my son Richard, whose interest, love, and support have always sustained me.

An important part of my life these days is babysitting for my two-year-old grandson, Desi, whose endless delight in all the wonders of the neighborhood—dandelions, puddles, worms, sparkly stones, a neighbor's chickens, feeding the birds, collecting sticks—fill me with joy and rekindle my own sense of wonder. Therefore, …

*I dedicate this book to*
**Desmond Joseph Pastor,**
*with love from Grammy.*

## I.

Autumn winds descend
to help maples relinquish
their late vanities.

**Broken Glass**

I have been dropping things:
a glass, a jar,
the clear lid to a pot.

The first two shattered,
shards of crystal thorns
that pierced my hands
as I gathered the swept mistakes.

The lid split like a frozen river:
sounds of rift and crackle
for several minutes
as I watched the damage scatter
small clear squares—safety glass—
that cut into knees and feet
nonetheless;
mosaics that clung to the soles of shoes
dispersed like a reminder
for days after.

Shards of pottery—ostraca—preserved in sand
were used for writing lessons in ancient Egypt.
These clear shards—made from sand—preserve nothing
but offer lessons in what I have lost.

I have been dropping things:
a glass, a jar, a lid,
my expectations about us,
my belief in solid form,
my need for clarity.

**Pottery Lesson**

> *It's not pots we are forming, it's ourselves.*
> *- M. C. Richards*

Sink thumbs into spheres of clay
and form pots:
vessels holding fingerprints
paddled into smooth
burnished into shine
and textured by coral.

Hand-building this is called
and mine are better formed now.
They cup in gracious acceptance
of these shapes.

I dream of the perfect tea bowl
worn by proffered hands
and grateful lips.
I look to the sky
wishing to press stars into this earth
and fire these pots with their impression.

Smoke the pots for stains of ash
that lick the inner surface dark
and wrap the form with shadows.
Cracks can be mended with spit
and burnished with stone.

Stars cannot be impressed
and pots unfired melt away
to earth.

**Vessel**

Woman,
you curve yourself
around, beneath,
to surround, to support,
to carve their needs into your bone.
You overflow to nourish dreams.

Your streams are panned for claims:
waters to cleanse
depths to fill
to reflect hope, swallow loss
and sift out grains of self.

Can you rescue their lives?
This boat is hewed from bone;
the sails are stretched like skin
straining to embrace them all.

**Fault Lines**

First the flaws are noticed:
a pimple or a misspelled word
the one grade not an A.
These subtract from the perfect whole.

When I was six,
we burned the word *can't*
in an ashtray on the kitchen table.
I understood the math: perfect = love.

Through years of chipped performance
cracked resolve
the crazed surface of ambition,
a pin hole in my offering dish widened
exposing unglazed clay
fired strong, unadorned:
*humble, simple, impermanent.*

The litany of "if only you were"
echoed through the cracks
until I understood the *wabi sabi* of repair.
A poet promised light through every crack.

A tea bowl falls and chips;
a hairline rift expands.
For past service and future promise
its brokenness is sealed with gold,
celebrating faults for what they are.

*Kintsugi is the Japanese practice of repairing broken pottery with gold.*

**Empty Nest**

Slender sticks extend
from branches bare and bleached
against a winter sky.

In a nook of twigs—
starched threads of cut lace—
a nest woven with urgency and art
lined with detritus
redefined for comfort:
lint and hair, shredded paper
feathers and tin foil,
tucked into leaks, patched with moss.

Dry deserted home:
fledglings gone,
the nesting pair have parted,
flown off in search of warmth.

**Empty Nest**

Slender sticks extend
from branches bare and bleached
against a winter sky.

In a nook of twigs—
starched threads of cut lace—
a nest woven with urgency and art
lined with detritus
redefined for comfort:
lint and hair, shredded paper
feathers and tin foil,
tucked into leaks, patched with moss.

Dry deserted home:
fledglings gone,
the nesting pair have parted,
flown off in search of warmth.

**Crows**

A cloud of crows
playfully scatter
across the sky
like children at recess.

Cawing loudly to each other
they holler and squawk
their disdain for the vees of geese
and laugh at non-corvids.

They land on naked branches,
notes on an unruly staff,
their presence an unexpected rest.

**That Fall**

*for Dad*

Was it the rank scent
of ginkgo fruit,
the constant litter of oaks,
the endless raking,
or the slow unwinding of crickets
that made you claim
you always hated Autumn?

Perhaps the earlier darkness
or the gradual chill?

So you left us as September broke
from Summer, replacing
the giddiness of back-to-school,
the wonder of reds and ochres
with the swirling eddy
of dying maple wings
that fall.

**October Metallurgy**

It's the maples that get you:
tomato red and ruby
still-green veins tipped in amber
plum and brass
copper, orange, sienna.
A joyful palette and such abundance!
Warm colors paint the sidewalks and lawns.
They hint at gold but tarnish,
crunch underfoot into base metals,
are swept away by winds and rakes.
Why each year is it such a surprise
that bare ebony trees line pewter lanes
and only glint with silver ice?

**November**

Crow song is not sweet
sawing over trees
grating stillness into alarm.
Dissonant solos
by blue-black observers
shred the silent fall of maple leaves
giving up for the year
and cancel the punctuation
of acorns underfoot.
These indigo informants
warn of what's to come—
dire, undecipherable
and dark.

## Japanese Maple in February

Tiny clenched fists joined by threads
cling to blackened twigs.
Crystal drips hang from the tips.
Withered old hands, crumpled paper paws,
twisted digits curled in awkward gestures:
unreleased during the fall of other leaves.
Why were these retained?
Reverence for age? nostalgia? indolence?
Or did you hate to let go of the gilded autumn
when garnet, amber, and citron replace
a palette of greens?

## Thaw

Rivulets of snowmelt
widen into sidewalk ponds,
channels urging
toward the sea-street.
Tufts of faded green are islands
in the drift.
Potholes are lakes.

Puffed out birds on bare branches
call to the warming breeze:
I need you I need you I need you.

Lighter days and coats,
the hunch of winter shoulders relaxed,
light reflecting off wet asphalt:
I watch the flow
listen for the next direction.

## II.

The hedge clipper song
of cicada crescendos:
autumn's approaching.

## Beachcombing

*Amelia Island, Florida*

I tell myself
"Just one more,"
then crouch and fill my pockets.
Each one is just
too perfect, too precious
to be left behind.
And I need to bring this place home.
How to pack
the early morning light
and sound of scumbling waves
the call of gulls
footprints of terns
the splash of diving pelicans?
So I pick up shells.

**Making Marks**

Marks that sing or fly
plead or march
shape notions
name feelings
form impulse into word.
They darken a page
and thoughts clarify:
butter in a glass--
hot golden liquid light--
casts shadows as it cools
and firms.
Inventing signs
that read the wind
and write the stars
I transcribe process
code meaning
mark time.

**Cicada Song**

Cicada song
swells and subsides:
crescendoed questions
awaiting replies.

Urgent wings saw
rolling waves of aria
crest through August skies
until summer's baton falls

silent.

**Psalm of Stone**

Melt, O God, this heart of stone
and re-ignite the magma
that cooled to solid core.
Like pumice filled with air,
lighten this density.

Split this heart of stone, O Lord,
and chip away the sparking flint,
the magnet ore,
the separate grains that merged to one.
Erode this stone
with facts and fragments
and reshape the nugget, Lord,
with patience
into gold.

Compress, O God, this heart of stone,
condense the space between us
and the time.
Forcing chalk into marble permanence,
pressing peat into coal,
You release heat, shed light.

If today I hear your voice,
harden not my heart.

## Shedding

Extra baggage accumulates in this life
a type of wealth
which overwhelms, imprisons, but inspires me
to lighten and unload,
to shed more than daily skin cells.

I'm at that point when outer layers
thin and sag
revealing strata that is calcified, condensed, or soft:
transparent hope, opaque mystery,
tender disappointment.

Leave outgrown skin behind.
Shed bark; expand limbs.
Molt: the itch of new feathers promises flight.

We're told to trim the fat, release
the inner child, expose essence,
strip away pretense,
shed inhibitions,
exfoliate.
So I pare down and peel off,
shred files, clear closets
and plane away curls of ragged grain.

Slough off acquired roles—
classroom mom, scout leader, hostess, maid, chauffeur—
to see the remains that once sufficed.
Wafers of mica, sliced from the whole, gain light.

Gather the excess.
Examine each layer.
Open your hand and let it go.

## My Yellow Room

*Ode to a 1950s childhood*

My yellow room is bright,
warm as buttered toast:
    brown and gold braided rug circles the floor
    --a road for little cars—
    and my red Victrola turns a 45.
    Roy and Dale sing "Happy Trails" to me
    as I color.

On my red table,
the crayon tin holds 96 colors:
    hundreds of pieces broken and sharpened,
    replenished on holidays.
    Periwinkle, magenta, sky blue, fuchsia,
    burnt sienna, copper and sea green
    are always worn down
    waxy paper jackets peeled away.
Crayola smells perfume the air.
I color in the lines and hum.

The toy hutch that Dad built
has narrow shelves on top for books:
    Golden books that I can reach;
    Childcraft, Lewis Carroll,
    *The Treasury* for bedtime stories.
The bottom shelves are deep and lined with boxes:
    paper dolls, seashells, Block City,
    dinosaurs, Disneykins, plastic apostles,
    and Betsy Wetsy, nestled in her case
    with change of clothes.

In one shoebox, amid the shells,
I've stashed a lambchop bone,

smuggled from dinner,
smooth and forbidden.

Pinky sits on my high bed,
a bear in yellow pajamas,
flanked by Tommy the Lion and Autograph Dog.
Under the bed at night flows the sea,
entombs the monsters, and holds the cave
where I join Peter to hide from Hook.

The tall dresser has six drawers
for undershirts and pants,
nighties, socks, and sweaters,
but the bottom drawer is mine,
where dress-up clothes are stored.
In Mom's silvery satin slip,
cast-off heels and poppette beads
I am Ginger Rogers.
In the cowgirl set, hula skirt, and tutu,
I join the adventures of Spin and Marty,
Shirley Temple, and the Mouseketeers.
I have a hat with ears.
And a magic wand.

For seven years this realm of only childhood
is safe from intrusion.
Imaginary friends and worlds are mine alone.
When "the baby" arrives,
my parents let me pick her middle name.
Mary Louise smiles at me
and I'm ready to share.

## Writing

Like a child's first drawings,
a line circles across the page, intent but random:
the ghostly doodles left by slugs
glow faintly on the morning sidewalk.
Most lines are punctuated
by the tiny curled body of the writer.

I wonder if these last silent messages record
a final burst of eloquence
a frantic call for help
a deathbed confession
or just the meandering trace
of a path to an ending,
a way to come to a full stop.

Sometimes, I embroider like that—
slow stitching it's called—
looking for direction in the weave of the cloth.
I want to express *flight*, remember *love*,
relate *loss*, or celebrate *reunion*,
without using letters.
I piece desires, regrets, and textures
with discursive threads
and punctuate the message with a knot.

## Autumn Litany

From the rank smell of ginkgo fruit
the departure of hummingbirds
the silence of cicadas
the return of mice under the stove
and overflowing gutters;
deliver me.

From ragweed and tree mold
pollen and dusty sneezes
deliver me.

For new school shoes and notebooks
softer sunshine and sweaters
the urgent preparation of squirrels
and the absence of mosquitoes;
I give thanks.

For the ticking clocks of crickets winding down
the mounds of mums
the twirling descent of maple wings
the crunching pop of acorn hats
and the satisfying shuffle through dry leaves;
I give thanks.

For the warm palette of decline,
the blend of red and green into maroon;
for every shade of crimson and vermilion,
citrine and ochre, amber, tangerine
and the richness of sepia, walnut, umber;
I give thanks.

For all this brilliant transition
I rejoice.

**Lessons**

These are the lessons of fall.

When you sense the end is coming,
respond with a song of color.

Give crimson, topaz, and bronze
to anyone who looks.

Rejoice in the green
that remains.

Hunker down and grow
smaller in awe of it all.

As cricket song fades, birds depart,
and blossoms clench into fists,
inhale the absence with gratitude
and

let it go.

## Getting Found

We carry maps within us that can be redrawn,
plotted to include a region once unknown,
marked with latitude and longitude lines
or the faces of sea monsters.

Our personal maps are colored by expectation,
limited by vision, expanded by imagination.
Some are worn thin, tattered by fingers tracing beyond
here and now; others crisply folded, pristine,
shelved by fear.

> *Some believe that quilts were used*
> *—symbolic blocks, stitches and knots—*
> *to map the route of fugitives*
> *on the Underground Railroad.*
> *Worn with use,*
> *there is no evidence.*

Direction suggests purpose, but is only movement:
progressive pulsing along a road or into the wild.
Meandering or marching, drifting or driving,
intention and attention converge from parallel paths.

Direction yields to happenstance—
a detour, a traffic jam, a glimpse of the sea—
and pursues decision over destination.
The notion of "from here to there" includes shifting boundaries,
changing scales, unmoored compass points,
if one is paying attention.

> *When planning roads through Central Park,*
> *Olmstead used desire lines*
> *—the paths that people want to walk—*
> *to recognize the routes.*

The lines on a map are not features of the land,
the textures, scents, or colors of a place described by a dot.

Marks on a musical score are not the sound,
emotion, tempo, or rhythm of music.
Definitions on a map—state park, alpine lake, plateau, marsh—
are suggestions on how to venture forth.
Scoring music and mapping place: marks on paper
that herald sound and promise arrival.

> *Aborigines inhabit the Dreaming,*
> *an imagined universe*
> *that connects with the world through songlines.*
> *Their song is the route; their map is musical.*

If the map I draw today identifies *terra incognita*,
realms with dragons, thorny woods, and quicksand
I know to stay within the lines and on the path.
It's when those place-names fade that boundaries shift,
expanses invite, and I can get my bearings,
change direction, and navigate the next route.

**Nest**

Black twigs against the winter blue
reveal a sort of basket in the crotch of a branch,
    withstanding wind and waiting
    for new tenants in the Spring.

Green-furred growth spreads up the limbs.
Robins build with moss and grass,
    dryer fluff, spider webs,
    string and feather down,
    plastic bags, squirrel hair,
    tinsel, mulch and stems.
Detritus weaves their comfort.

The nesting pair warms their eggs,
    listens for cracks,
    observes each struggle to hatch.
They nurture the yawping naked nuggets:
    all need and noise and promise.

**Last Walk**

Last walk of the day,
the dog and I venture into the drizzle.
A raindrop clings to every twig of the dead maple.
A street lamp transforms that skeleton
into a filigree chandelier.
It sheds heavy tears of light
onto pavement and into the street
slightly warmed by early March
so that oil stains are rainbows
and a chore becomes a stroll.

**Extension**

I am seated, chaired to indecision.
Your words flow strong
like grains of oak.
They touch me,
fragile and dry as twigs of coral.

I am connected fragments:
foot in shoe on plank
that leads to wall
and corner lines to ceiling.
I am land alone.
You drift to build an isthmus.

The wood will turn to sea
if I step out.
Before I trust the undertow
show me you are rock.

**Our Garden**

We chose the seeds
and counted spaces for them.
On hands and knees
we marked corners with stones
and dug with claw tools and spades.
Scraping pebbles, winter thatch
and greening clods
we smiled at our patch of dust
pretending we were farmers
and this land our office.

Dumping peat and compost,
we bleached our hands with lime
and sifted all the browns
through our fingers.
We played at smelling the soil:
"More lime," we agreed.

Packets holding promises
of eggplants and string beans
were opened and the grains
of crops were counted.
We stifled our desire for abundance
and planted seeds in proper rows
and mounds requiring distance.
Then it rained with hoses and sprinklers.

Sitting back on our heels
we watched.
Tomorrow we'd return to desks
but this day we had tilled our earth
and had together grown.

**Spring Inspiration**

Breathe in the spirit:
drops of air
seeds of color and shadow
pollen of ideas.

Spring is
the calligraphy of yearning vines
the Braille of budding twigs
the song of rain and silk
scarves of breeze
lace parasol of tiny maple leaves
a quiet alert of red tulips.

Nourished by these fragments
I construct a map
that shows me how to proceed.

Eventually
I exhale a response:
words and shapes
describe where I am.

**As the Crow Flies**

In a direction yet to be determined
I flutter around in search
of good works, easy answers,
and time.

The crow atop a sycamore
eyes me walking the dog
and calls: a greeting?
a warning? advice?
Then flies off, leaving
a faint gray line in the sky
because one of my eyes is blurry.

I follow the line until it's gone;
the dog waits patiently.
My daily prayer sends out thanks
for these encounters.

Appreciation is the key
but which lock am I picking?
Maybe patience is the key.

All I know is that at this age
there are more questions than answers
and more memories than plans.
Scanning obituaries for clues
to my estimated time of departure,
I find comfort alongside fear.

And so much longing,
for a do-over, a change of venue,
a different set of talents.
The faint gray trail I'm leaving
is graphite, ink, paper, and words
that will fade in time.
As the crow flies to a higher perch,
I ask for ascent and clarity.

## About the Author

Born in 1952 in Teaneck, NJ, Meg Kennedy graduated from the College of Notre Dame of Maryland (now the University of Notre Dame of Maryland) and worked as a promotional writer in the marketing departments of several university presses for more than twenty years. During that time her interest and ability in calligraphy and bookbinding grew. Since leaving her last office job, she worked as a freelance artist and instructor at community art centers in the Delaware Valley, served as an artist-in-residence at numerous schools in Pennsylvania and New Jersey, and conducted workshops at Swarthmore College, Drexel University, Kutztown University, Villanova University, and the Philadelphia Museum of Art. She lives with her husband in Wynnewood, PA.

www.ingramcontent.com/pod-product-compliance
Lightning Source LLC
Chambersburg PA
CBHW042350040426
42449CB00018B/3473